WORK, BUT THIS TIME LIKE YOU MEAN IT

BY HONOR WEBSTER-MANNISON

CURRENT THEATRE SERIES

First published in 2024
by Currency Press Pty Ltd,
Gadigal Land, Suite 310, 46–56 Kippax Street, Surry Hills, NSW 2010, Australia
enquiries@currency.com.au
www.currency.com.au

in association with Canberra Youth Theatre

Typeset by Brighton Gray for Currency Press.
Printed by Fineline Print + Copy Services, Revesby, NSW.
Cover shows Isaiah Prichard; photograph by Adam McGrath.

Currency Press acknowledges the Traditional Owners of the Country on which we live and work. We pay our respects to all Aboriginal and Torres Strait Islander Elders, past and present.

A catalogue record for this book is available from the National Library of Australia

Contents

Work, But This Time Like You Mean It was commissioned and first produced by Canberra Youth Theatre at The Courtyard Studio, Canberra Theatre Centre, Ngunnawal Land, on 20 September 2024, with the following cast:

SHIFT MANAGER	Tom Bryson
DRIVE	Quinn Goodwin
FOOD PREP	Sterling Notley
DEEP FRYER	Matthew Hogan
REGISTER ONE	Kathleen Dunkerley
REGISTER TWO	Emma Piva
KIOSK	Georgie Bianchini
REGULAR	Hannah Cornelia

Director, Luke Rogers
Set and Costume Designer, Kathleen Kershaw
Lighting and Video Designer, Ethan Hamill
Sound Designer and Composer, Patrick Haesler
Production Stage Manager, Rhiley Winnett

Honor Webster-Mannison was the winner of the 2022 Emerging Playwright Commission, generously supported by Holding Redlich.

CHARACTERS

SHIFT MANAGER, 18. Is sometimes referred to as Mike.

DRIVE, 21.

FOOD PREP, 15.

DEEP-FRYER, 17.

REGULAR, 17. Is drinking a frozen Mountain Dew.

REGISTER ONE, 16. Is on the phone.

REGISTER TWO, 16. Is running late.

KIOSK, 13. Is sometimes referred to as Fifi.

CHARACTERS PLAYED BY OTHER CHARACTERS

OFFICE WORKER ONE

OFFICE WORKER TWO

BOSS

MARKET RESEARCHER

DEEP FRYER'S MUM

CUSTOMER

LITERAL DEEP-FRYER, or this could be voiceover, projection, etc.

GENERAL MANAGER

Note: characters' pronouns referenced in the play can be changed.

NOTES ON ACTION

The work being performed throughout the play should be real work: activity involving mental or physical effort done in order to achieve a purpose or result.

NOTES ON TEXT

Dialogue in **bold** means that it's said simultaneously or overlapping.

— indicates an interruption, or breaking-off of thought.

/ indicates the line interrupts the line before it.

… indicates a trailing off of thought or a pause.

An indent indicates that the dialogue is taking place in a different area of the restaurant:

front of house and drive-thru

        kitchen

                bins

CONTENT WARNING

Gory bits.

This play text went to press before the end of rehearsals and may differ from the play as performed.

BEFORE THE PLAY

As the audience is being seated, the performers are operating as a well-oiled machine, working their butts off, earning their money, pushing through, pumping it out, moving on up, work bitch work.

KIOSK *reads from their employee handbook.*

KIOSK: One. Be your best self.

Beat.

Two. Trust.

Beat.

Three. Pride.

Beat.

Four. Safety.

Beat.

Five. Have fun.

The title of the play, which is also the title of the first scene, is projected.

WORK, BUT THIS TIME LIKE YOU MEAN IT

The time is 7:48 p.m. The same nothing song plays. REGISTER TWO *is running late.*

KIOSK: **Five. Have fun.**

KIOSK *exits.*

DRIVE: **Hi, thanks for waiting. What can I get you?**
REGISTER ONE: **Hi, thanks for waiting. What can I get you?**
SHIFT MANAGER: How are the tenders going?
DRIVE: **I've got the Ultimate Box.**
REGISTER ONE: **I've got the Super Nugget Combo.**
DEEP-FRYER: Golden. Chef's kiss. Double shakas—

DRIVE: / **Would you like a drink with that?**

REGISTER ONE: / **Would you like a drink with that?**

SHIFT MANAGER: Order one-four-eight.

DRIVE: Please proceed to the **next window.**

REGISTER ONE: **Tap the top** when you're ready.

DEEP-FRYER: I'm gonna set a mattress on fire after work.

FOOD PREP: What.

DEEP-FRYER: I'm gonna set a mattress on fire.

DRIVE: That will be thirteen ninety-five. **Thanks. Have a good night.**

REGISTER ONE: **Thanks. Have a good night.**

DRIVE: Hi, thanks for waiting. What can I get you?

FOOD PREP: You're not.

DEEP-FRYER: I got all the materials.

DRIVE: So I've got the bacon and cheese burger.

REGULAR: Hey, is my tongue green?

DRIVE: Do you want that in a meal?

REGISTER ONE: Pretty green yeah.

REGULAR: It really actually really sucks.

REGISTER ONE: **Yeah.**

DRIVE: **Pepsi Max.**

KIOSK *enters and goes to kitchen.*

SHIFT MANAGER: Order one-four-nine.

DEEP-FRYER: **Matches, sparklers, kerosene …**

DRIVE: **Please proceed to the next window.**

SHIFT MANAGER: Order one-fifty.

FOOD PREP: Mike, there's a rando kid in the kitchen.

SHIFT MANAGER: What?

DEEP-FRYER: Rando kid wearing a uniform in the kitchen.

REGULAR: And the after-party was gonna be massive. There was gonna be a jumping castle.

KIOSK: I'm new.

SHIFT MANAGER: That's umm … umm …

SHIFT MANAGER *reads* KIOSK*'s name badge.*

SHIFT MANAGER: Fifi. Fifi's training. [*to* KIOSK] You've read the handbook?

DEEP-FRYER: No offence but Fifi looks five.

REGULAR: And memories.

SHIFT MANAGER: Well Fifi's not five, Fifi's …

KIOSK: Thirteen.

FOOD PREP: Sounds illegal.

DEEP-FRYER: Legit.

DRIVE: Twelve ninety-five.

SHIFT MANAGER: It's not illegal.

REGULAR: And experiences.

SHIFT MANAGER: If your parents sign a form it's not illegal.

REGULAR: **Are you listening?**

DRIVE: **Have a great day.**

SHIFT MANAGER: [*to* KIOSK] So you'll mainly be on our self-service kiosks.

REGISTER ONE: There's a job going at DFO Grill'd.

DRIVE: [*to* FOOD PREP] Can you help me with the bins?

FOOD PREP: Sure.

FOOD PREP *and* DRIVE *take out the bins.*

REGISTER TWO *enters.*

REGISTER TWO: [*to* SHIFT MANAGER] So so so so so so sorry I'm late.

SHIFT MANAGER: [*to* KIOSK] Just wait here.

REGISTER TWO: I swear I will never be late again. I swear it on my mother's **life. And I promise to be dedicated, committed, hard working, pour everything I have into this job and be so dedicated and punctual and …**

REGULAR: **Okay, so … I'm meant to go to Andy's house for pres and then my mum is looking through my bag, like absolutely paranoid, and she finds a flask, but most parents are buying their kids drinks right.** You know Andy?

SHIFT MANAGER: Remember **five minutes early is …**

REGISTER TWO: **Five minutes … is …**

FOOD PREP *and* DRIVE *come back from taking out the bins.*

DRIVE: Hi, thanks for waiting. What can I get for you today?

DEEP-FRYER: Look. Burger-bun boobs.

SHIFT MANAGER: Is …

REGISTER TWO: Is …

DEEP-FRYER: **Look.**

DRIVE: **Sorry.** I can't hear you.

SHIFT MANAGER: On Ttttiii**mmmeee.**

REGISTER TWO: **Time. On time.**

DEEP-FRYER: Like little pillows.

FOOD PREP: Lol.

DRIVE: Move closer. Move closer to the speaker thing.

SHIFT MANAGER: And on time is …

REGISTER TWO: Is not **on time.**

SHIFT MANAGER: **Is late.** Thank you.

REGISTER ONE: Sorry I didn't see you.

SHIFT MANAGER: Can I get order one-five-eight. Order one-five-nine.

REGISTER TWO: **What did I miss?**

REGISTER ONE: **What would you like?**

REGULAR: Formal.

Beeping.

FOOD PREP: Something's beeping?

DRIVE: Sorry but I can't **hear you.**

DEEP-FRYER: **Fuck …** I forgot about the tenders.

REGISTER ONE: We don't do coffee.

REGISTER TWO: I wouldn't go to a private school formal, **mate.**

FOOD PREP: **Mate.**

REGISTER ONE: Macca's does coffee.

REGISTER TWO: Limos.

FOOD PREP: We're outta burger buns.

REGISTER TWO: RM's.

DEEP-FRYER: **There's a box on the …**

FOOD PREP: **Where's the mini knifey** thing?

REGISTER TWO: … those straw hats that make you look like Anne of Green Cables.

REGULAR: Gables.

SHIFT MANAGER: What's happening **with order one-five-one?**

FOOD PREP: / **Yeah sorry, I'm** just getting some more buns because—

REGISTER TWO: Really nice mums but.

SHIFT MANAGER: We need to be moving **faster.**

FOOD PREP: **Yep.**

REGISTER TWO: Type of mums that give you a blanky and choccy milk.

REGULAR: **What are you talking about.**

REGISTER ONE: **Mike, a customer wants to talk to you.**

SHIFT MANAGER: We're really behind tonight, team. We need to pick up the pace.

DRIVE: **Hi, thanks for waiting. What can I get for you?**

REGISTER ONE: **Hi, thanks for waiting. What can I get for you?**

REGISTER TWO: **Hi, thanks for waiting. What can I get for you?**

FOOD PREP: Something's beeping?

DEEP-FRYER: Fuck … I forgot about the tenders.

REGISTER TWO: Unfortunately we don't have the Twister anymore.

SHIFT MANAGER: What's happening **with order one-five-one—**

FOOD PREP: / **Yeah sorry, I'm** just getting some more buns—

REGISTER ONE: **Mike. Hello. Mike.**

REGISTER TWO: **I know it's totally devastating.**

SHIFT MANAGER: In a minute. Someone can't open a **frickin'** box of bread.

DEEP-FRYER: **Whoa.**

Beeping stops.

KIOSK *and* REGISTER TWO *exit.*

DRIVE: **Hi, thanks for waiting. What can I get you?**

REGISTER ONE: **Hi, thanks for waiting. What can I get you?**

SHIFT MANAGER: How are the tenders going?

DRIVE: **I've got the Ultimate Box.**

REGISTER ONE: **I've got the Super Nugget Combo.**

DEEP-FRYER: Golden. Chef's kiss. Double shakas—

DRIVE: / **Would you like a drink with that?**

REGISTER ONE: / **Would you like a drink with that?**

SHIFT MANAGER: Order one-four-eight.

DRIVE: Please proceed to the **next window.**

REGISTER ONE: **Tap the top** when you're ready.

REGISTER ONE: I'd rather be at Grill'd. Grill'd is way less greasy and disgusting.

REGULAR: I can see you there.

DEEP-FRYER: I'm gonna set a mattress on fire. Matches, sparklers, kerosene—

DRIVE: **Have a great night.**

REGISTER ONE: **Have a great night.**

FOOD PREP: / What if it exploded.

DEEP-FRYER: Bro.

FOOD PREP: Booo**oom …**

DEEP-FRYER: **Booow**ooooffff … Noooo my eyes.

Shllllth … metal mattress spring … piercing … through … heart …

FOOD PREP: Dude, no. No you can't.

REGULAR: Is my tongue green?

REGISTER ONE: Pretty green, yeah.

REGULAR: This is my seventh Mountain Dew Freeze. I'm gonna shit myself.

SHIFT MANAGER: Order one-fifty.

KIOSK *enters and goes to kitchen.*

FOOD PREP: Mike, there's a rando kid in the kitchen.

SHIFT MANAGER: What?

DEEP-FRYER: Rando kid wearing a uniform in the kitchen.

FOOD PREP: Way too young to witness what's going on here.

DEEP-FRYER: It's carnage.

FOOD PREP: Complete carnage, chaos, graphic violence.

KIOSK: I'm new.

SHIFT MANAGER: That's umm … umm …

SHIFT MANAGER *reads* KIOSK*s name badge.*

KIOSK: F—

SHIFT MANAGER: / Fifi. Fifi's training. [*to* KIOSK] You've read the handbook?

KIOSK *nods head yes.*

SHIFT MANAGER: Do you have any questions?

KIOSK *shakes head no.*

SHIFT MANAGER: Great. So right now we're in the kitchen and the kitchen is where the food gets made.

DEEP-FRYER: [*to* KIOSK] Bad things happen here.
FOOD PREP: Leave this place while you still have time.
DRIVE: Hey, can you help me with the bins?
FOOD PREP: Sure.

FOOD PREP *and* DRIVE *take out the bins.*

SHIFT MANAGER: Ignore them.

KIOSK *nods head yes.*

Let's keep moving towards front of house.

REGISTER TWO *enters.*

REGISTER TWO: So so so so so so sorry I'm late—
SHIFT MANAGER: / I hate to do this, but I am going to have to give you a **final warning.**

DRIVE: **I think I'm depressed.**
FOOD PREP: You don't look depressed.
DRIVE: Really.
FOOD PREP: Yeah. You look great.
DRIVE: I just feel like I'm almost twenty-two and I'm wearing the same uniform that I've had since I was sixteen and all that's changed is … nothing's changed.

REGISTER TWO: I swear I will never be late again. I swear it on my mother's **life. And I promise to be dedicated, committed, hard working, pour everything I have into this job and be so dedicated and punctual and …**
REGULAR: **Okay so … I'm meant to go to Andy's house for pre's and then my mum is looking through my bag, like absolutely paranoid, and she finds a flask, but most parents are buying their kids drinks right.** You know Andy?

DRIVE: You know how they put cameras in the freezer?
FOOD PREP: You got your nose pierced [*or something that's relevant to the performer*]. That's a change.
DRIVE: That was my cry spot.

FOOD PREP: What's a cry spot?

DRIVE: A place where you cry and nobody sees you.
Everybody has a cry spot.

FOOD PREP: I don't think they do.

DRIVE: They do.

FOOD PREP: I mean I don't have a cry spot.
Aren't you meant to be on drive?

DRIVE: It's fine, I've got the headset thingy.

SHIFT MANAGER: Remember five **minutes early is …**

REGISTER TWO: **Five minutes … is …**

SHIFT MANAGER: **Is …**

REGISTER TWO: **Is …**

FOOD PREP: I better get back.

FOOD PREP *and* DRIVE *come back from taking out the bins.*

DRIVE: Hi, thanks for waiting. What can I get for you today?

DEEP-FRYER: Look. Burger-bun boobs.

REGISTER TWO: Is not **on time.**

SHIFT MANAGER: **Is late.** Thank you.

DEEP-FRYER: Like little pillows.

REGISTER ONE: Sorry I didn't see you.

FOOD PREP: Lol.

DEEP-FRYER: Whoa, buns are like pillows for burgers.

SHIFT MANAGER: [*to* KIOSK] It's really important that you arrive ten minutes before your shift starts. Are you … how are you getting to work?

KIOSK: My mum's dropping me.

REGISTER TWO: **What did I miss?**

REGISTER ONE: **What would you like?**
We don't do coffee.

Beeping.

FOOD PREP: Something's beeping.

DEEP-FRYER: Fuck. I forgot about the tenders.

REGISTER ONE: We don't do coffee. Macca's does coffee.

REGISTER TWO: **You know what it's gonna be …**

FOOD PREP: **We're outta burger buns.**

DEEP-FRYER: There's a box above your head.

REGISTER TWO: Hi, thanks for waiting. **What can I get for you?**

FOOD PREP: **Where's the mini knifey thing?**

REGISTER TWO: Unfortunately we don't have the Twister anymore. I've contacted them about it.

SHIFT MANAGER: What's happening **with order one-five-one—**

FOOD PREP: / **Yeah sorry, I'm** just getting some more buns—

REGISTER ONE: Mike. Hello. **Mike.**

REGISTER TWO: **I know** it's totally devastating.

SHIFT MANAGER: In a minute. Someone can't open a **frickin'** box of bread.

DEEP-FRYER: **Whoa.**

REGISTER ONE: **Mike.**

DEEP-FRYER: **Mike**, there's kids around.

KIOSK: I'm thirteen.

Beeping stops.

REGISTER ONE: **Hi, thanks for waiting. What can I get you?**

DRIVE: **Hi, thanks for waiting. What can I get you?**

REGISTER ONE: I shouldn't be here and everyone knows it. I should be at Grill'd. Grill'd DFO. I'd never go on Roaccutane if I was at Grill'd. I have a recurring fantasy and this is it. I'm working drive. A customer asks me how many pieces of chicken are in a Ten Piece Bucket. I have this fuck-off Samurai sword. I open the car door. The driver falls to their knees. They're begging. Really begging. I slnnnng. Just beheading them all. The whole drive-thru. Blood spraying on the window. I have this look in my eyes that is like measured, unfeeling, I feel nothing—

DRIVE: / What would you like for your first side?

REGISTER TWO: It's seven forty-eight and my shift started at seven thirty and I'm on my way to work and I can't stop thinking about—

REGISTER ONE: / I'm glistening.

REGISTER TWO: That time I bleached your hair and it went like cobwebs, like barbie doll hair when you wash it with dish soap.

REGISTER ONE: My whole body is glistening and shining and coated in …

Also, Grill'd uniforms are way nicer. Also, you don't get fired on your eighteenth birthday.
I got my period. And I didn't have like … like any of the stuff … because you know … I'm dumb. So I got toilet paper and rolled it into a wad and then used more toilet paper to tie the wad to my undies and I can feel the blood soaking through all of it. I can feel it soaking through the toilet paper, the undies, the pants, everything. So gross. Like why don't they have a box of tampons in the bathroom. Because this place is cheap.

REGISTER TWO: After work we sit in your car in the car park and wait for nothing. We're gonna grow up in car parks. In your dad's car. I like it when you waste time.
And there was that song like …

REGISTER TWO *hums a bit of the song.*

REGISTER ONE *hums a bit of the song.*

REGISTER TWO *and* REGISTER ONE *are in a car.*

REGISTER ONE: I hate this song. You know I'm bi. I haven't told Milo yet. He'd be completely fine with it.

REGISTER TWO: Yeah. I mean … why wouldn't he be fine with it?

REGISTER ONE: Everyone's a bit bi anyway.

REGISTER TWO: Yeah. Yeah.
Sometimes we'd wait in the car outside of Macca's for Milo to go on break. Like we'd wait in the car for his whole shift. Like we'd drive him there and then we'd wait and then we'd drive him home. You got so mad when I called you the Burger King and Queen. How do you like know?

REGISTER ONE: It's just something you know. I'm so bored. I swear nothing's on anymore—

REGULAR *knocks on the car window.*

REGISTER TWO: / **What the …**

REGISTER ONE: **Jesus Christ.**

REGULAR: **Hey.**

REGISTER TWO: Jesus. I thought you were a psycho serial killer.

REGULAR: Just me.

REGISTER ONE: What are you doing here?
REGULAR: Looking for you.
REGISTER ONE: How did you know we were here?
REGULAR: I know your roster.
REGISTER ONE: You are such a stalker.
REGISTER TWO: I thought you were at Becca's house.
REGULAR: We were but then Becca's mum kicked us out because— Oh my fucking god, did you know their house is like full of cats. They have so many cats, it's literally insane.
REGISTER ONE: Becca looks a bit like a cat.
Can you not drink that in my car?
REGULAR: Oh come on.
REGISTER ONE: I don't want you to spill it.
REGULAR: Okay.
I saw you eating in the car the other day, but okay it's fine.
REGISTER ONE: But I don't spill things.

DRIVE *and* FOOD PREP *take out the bins.*

DRIVE: It's lonely.
REGULAR: That's rude.
DRIVE: Reaching out with your EFTPOS stick.
REGISTER ONE: It's not rude, it's just true.
REGISTER TWO: You know what else is true?
DRIVE: It sounds like a hospital.
REGISTER TWO: That someone found a brain in their fried chicken the other day.
REGISTER ONE: That is not true.
REGULAR: Who told you that?
REGISTER TWO: You know the girl who looks scared all the time, works Mondays. She told me.
REGULAR: Oh my god, I actually saw this online. It's not a brain it's—
REGISTER TWO: / It's fully brain.
REGISTER ONE: It wasn't brain.
REGISTER TWO: **I swear.**
REGULAR: **It's kidney.**
I saw this online.
It looks like brain but it's actually kidney.

DRIVE: It's just like what am I doing? What are you doing?

FOOD PREP: I work here.

DRIVE: For the rest of your life?

FOOD PREP: Probably till I'm twenty.

DRIVE: I'm almost twenty-two.

FOOD PREP: Oh. I thought you were seventeen.

DRIVE: This job makes me feel old at twenty-two.

FOOD PREP: I think you're catastrophising. Work's not that bad.

DRIVE: Work's giving me depression.

FOOD PREP: The people are great.

DRIVE: I feel like it's sucking out my soul.

FOOD PREP: Have you heard of compartmentalisation?

DRIVE: If you don't use your brain to do smart things, your cells die. I pretend I know what compartmentalisation means but I actually have no idea.

FOOD PREP: Work time is work time, home time is home time and social time is social time.

DRIVE: But what does that actually even mean?

FOOD PREP: What do you like to do outside of work?

DRIVE: I watch TV. What do you do?

FOOD PREP: I play the oboe.

Beeping. FOOD PREP *and* DRIVE *come back from taking out the bins.*

REGISTER TWO: Hi, thanks for waiting. What can I get for you? Unfortunately we don't have the Twister anymore.

Beat.

It was our best burger option by far.

Beat.

Oh trust me, I've contacted them about it.

SHIFT MANAGER: What's happening with order one-five-one?
REGISTER ONE: **Mike. Hello. Mike.**
REGISTER TWO: **I know it's devastating.**
SHIFT MANAGER: In a minute. Someone can't open a **frickin'** box of bread.
DEEP-FRYER: **Whoa.** Mike, there's kids around.
KIOSK: I'm thirteen.

Beeping stops.

DEEP-FRYER: **This is fucked in the head. This is totally fucked in the head.**
DRIVE: **This is fucked in the head. This is totally fucked in the head.**

A REST BREAK ALLOWS AN EMPLOYEE TO REST FOR A SHORT PERIOD OF TIME DURING WORK HOURS

An air horn blows which means the performers have a break.

Everyone scrolls ...

Everyone scrolls and scrolls and scrolls and scrolls and scrolls ...

and laughs ...

and scrolls ...

Beat.

Everyone drinks some water, maybe has a little snack if they brought one

and scrolls.

Beat.

There is the sound of an air horn, which means we resume.

WORK, BUT THIS TIME WITH FEELING

The time is 7:48 p.m. The same nothing song plays.

REGISTER ONE *is still scrolling.*

REGISTER ONE: Hi, thanks for waiting. What can I get you?

Beat.

Super Nugget Combo.

Beat.

Would you like a drink with that?

Beat.

Tap when you're ready.

Beat.

Up the top.

Beat.

Thanks, have a good—

REGULAR: / Hey is my tongue green?

REGISTER ONE: Pretty green, yeah.

REGULAR: It really actually really sucks.

REGISTER ONE: —

REGULAR: That I can't go.

REGISTER ONE: —

REGULAR: I can't go to my formal.

REGISTER ONE: —

REGULAR: Everyone will have pictures and have made new memories and …

REGISTER ONE: —

REGULAR: Like, except I—

REGISTER ONE *laughs at something on their phone.*

Are you listening?

REGISTER ONE: Were you talking?

REGULAR: Oh my god.

REGISTER ONE: I struggle to concentrate when you talk.

REGULAR: Okay, so … I'm meant to go to Andy's house for pre's and then my mum is looking through my bag, like absolutely paranoid, and she finds a flask, but most parents are buying their kids drinks right? Do you know Andy? Like a very face face. And my mum just fully loses it and is like, she's been so over the top since the whole curtains incident, anyway she's like you need to be shown that your actions have consequences.

REGISTER ONE: There's a job going at DFO Grill'd.

REGULAR: I know my actions have consequences. But also her actions have consequences.

REGISTER ONE: —

REGULAR: Like do you hate your kid?

REGISTER ONE: I can imagine hating my kid.

REGULAR: Like, does she actually hate me?
Do I look like I've been crying?

REGISTER ONE: You always look like you've been crying.

REGULAR: That was in grade three.

REGISTER ONE: Pink eye.

REGULAR: It wasn't pink eye.

REGISTER ONE: Are you going to the after-party?

REGULAR: No, because Andy's mum is like mum-friends with my mum and they'd definitely—

REGISTER ONE: / Sad.
Sorry I didn't see you there.

REGULAR: And I had this feeling like deep, deep, deep—

Beeping.

REGISTER ONE: / What would you like?

REGULAR: ... deep, deep—

REGISTER ONE: / Sorry we don't do coffee.

REGULAR: ... inside my bones
That this night was gonna be like ...

REGISTER ONE: Macca's does coffee.
Mike, a customer wants to talk to you.

Beeping stops.

SHIFT MANAGER: I guess right now, the moment before it happened, I'm staring at the order screen and there's a little square, on the order screen, a little square that shows us our KPIs, that's short for key performance indicator, or I guess it would be key performance indicators with an s.
I'm staring at our KPI box, the KPIs for the store, I'm staring at it and ...
It's not good.

It's not bad.
It's definitely not as good as yesterday's.
I think Maria was the shift manager on yesterday.
Which always makes me a bit, not stressed, but tense. Definitely tense.

Beat.

I sometimes, actually very frequently, actually all the time, imagine that I'm in an office.
Just to calm down.
I'm in an office.
And instead of the counter, there's desks and cubicle walls. And instead of tiles there's grey carpet.
And instead of the drinks fridge, there's a water-cooler. And there's those white plastic cups.
For the water.
For the water that you get from the water cooler. And I have a tie. And I have a team. But nothing like this team. This is a team of office workers.
And I have an ergonomic chair and an ergonomic keyboard and an ergonomic mouse. And someone, maybe someone from my team, but someone says—

DEEP-FRYER *becomes* OFFICE WORKER ONE. *The same nothing song becomes an office version of the same nothing song. The time is now 7:48 a.m.*

OFFICE WORKER ONE: Hey Mike. How was your weekend?
SHIFT MANAGER: I took the kids kayaking.
OFFICE WORKER ONE: Wow, you have kids.
SHIFT MANAGER: Yeah.
OFFICE WORKER ONE: Me and the lads were thinking of sinking some pints at the pub after work. You should join.
SHIFT MANAGER: I wish.
This report won't write itself.
OFFICE WORKER ONE: No rest for the wicked.
SHIFT MANAGER: No rest for the wicked. Anyways, I'm sure you lads wouldn't want your boss hanging around while you're trying to let—

OFFICE WORKER ONE: / Shut up Mike.

Beat.

You know we don't see you like that.

SHIFT MANAGER: Sounds—

OFFICE WORKER ONE: / Anyway, better get back to the ol' desk …

Beat.

Look, I probably shouldn't say this but …

SHIFT MANAGER: What?

OFFICE WORKER ONE: No, I shouldn't. You seem stressed.

SHIFT MANAGER: Really?

OFFICE WORKER ONE: You seem stressed out bro. And you shouldn't be. Because word around here is you're about to— [*Miming shooting a hoop*] score a pr-pr-pr-promotion.

SHIFT MANAGER: Of course there'd be people higher up than me. It's a large company after all. There'd be a b—

KIOSK *becomes* BOSS.

BOSS: / As the boss of this company I can see that you have a lot of potential Mike. That's exactly what we want to see in someone in an executive assistant project managerial position like yourself.

DRIVE *becomes* OFFICE WORKER TWO.

OFFICE WORKER TWO: Well … well … well … what's going on here. Working hard or hardly working.

OFFICE WORKER ONE: You know … just catchin' … catchin' up. I was just saying Mark here should—

SHIFT MANAGER: / It's Mike.

OFFICE WORKER ONE: Yeah. Anyway, I gotta go do some photocopying and—

OFFICE WORKER TWO: / So Mike, I wanted to tell you … Look at me now, I'm embarrassed … I just wanted to … ummm … just tell you how … oh god, why am I so embarrassed by this. Okay, like I just wanted to say how sexy and confident I think you are. Do you swim—

REGULAR: / This is my seventh Mountain Dew Freeze. I think I'm gonna shit myself.

OFFICE WORKER TWO: Do you swim?

SHIFT MANAGER: One-four-eight. I mean, sorry … I mean, yeah I swim. [*To* REGULAR] Do you work here? You can't be here if you don't work here.

REGULAR: Well, I'm meant to be at my formal tonight so …

Beeping.

REGISTER ONE: **Mike. Hello. Mike.**

REGISTER TWO: **I know it's devastating.**

REGULAR: **I know it's devastating.**

SHIFT MANAGER: Sorry, what were you saying?

REGISTER ONE: Mike. Hello Mike, a customer **wants to talk to you.**

SHIFT MANAGER: **About swimming?**

REGISTER ONE: They want a coffee.

SHIFT MANAGER: We don't do coffee.

REGISTER ONE: Can you tell them that?

Beeping stops.

The song returns to the same nothing song, rather than the office version of the same nothing song.

DRIVE: **Hi, thanks for waiting. What can I get you?**

REGISTER ONE: **Hi, thanks for waiting. What can I get you?**

SHIFT MANAGER: How are the tenders going?

DRIVE: **I've got the Ultimate Box.**

REGISTER ONE: **I've got the Super Nugget Combo.**

DEEP-FRYER: Golden. Chef's kiss. Double shakas—

DRIVE: / **Would you like a drink with that?**

REGISTER ONE: / **Would you like a drink with that?**

SHIFT MANAGER: Order one-four-eight.

DRIVE: Please proceed to the **next window.**

REGISTER ONE: **Tap the top** when you're ready.

DEEP-FRYER: I'm gonna set a mattress on fire after work.

FOOD PREP: What?

DEEP-FRYER: I'm gonna set a mattress on fire.

DRIVE: I'm sorry, did you say **Pepsi?**

SHIFT MANAGER: **Order one-four-six.**

REGULAR: I'm actually really sensitive about the whole pink eye thing. I don't bring up the fact that you—

REGISTER ONE: / I've got to tell kitchen something.

REGISTER ONE *goes to the kitchen.*

DEEP-FRYER: Matches, sparklers—

REGISTER ONE: [*to* DEEP-FRYER] / You messed up order one-four-eight.
You gave them coleslaw instead of mash.

DEEP-FRYER: That's not my department, soooo. [*To* FOOD PREP] You are the one that has messed up order one-four-eight.

REGISTER ONE: Well, maybe if you stop fucking around, we can all go home on time tonight.

DEEP-FRYER: Keep making up all these excuses to come to the kitchen and visit—

REGISTER ONE: / I find you repulsive.

REGISTER ONE *returns to Front Counter.*

DEEP-FRYER: I swear front's always accusing us.

FOOD PREP: Dealing with customers though—

DEEP-FRYER: / Are you kidding. They just sit with their phones under the counter like this … that's legit all they do.

FOOD PREP: Sorry man, I'm slack tonight or—

DEEP-FRYER: / Never apologise. Front's the weakest link. Literally I could do their job twice as fast as them. So the mattress burning you in or out?

FOOD PREP: I'm pretty wrecked.

DEEP-FRYER: You wanna dexie?

FOOD PREP: I'm good. Do mattresses explode?

DEEP-FRYER: Dude.

FOOD PREP: Booo**ooom …**

DEEP-FRYER: **Booow**ooooffff …

FOOD PREP: Protect the young.

DEEP-FRYER: [*to* KIOSK] Save the children.

FOOD PREP: [*to* KIOSK] Shield your eyes.

Sound of muffled explosion.

FOOD PREP: Noooooooo. Duuuuuudddeee.

DEEP-FRYER: Shllllth … metal mattress spring … piercing … through … heart …

FOOD PREP: No you can't— You
Nooooooo.
You put the nuggets in?

DEEP-FRYER: Oh yeah they're done. So, are you coming?

FOOD PREP: It sounds like you really want me there.

DEEP-FRYER: I'm in a relationship.

FOOD PREP: That's bullshit.

DEEP-FRYER: Sorry to disappoint. She works here.

FOOD PREP: Who?

DEEP-FRYER: You don't believe me. I'll show you the texts.

FOOD PREP: You're delusional.

DEEP-FRYER: I've got the texts.

FOOD PREP: Is she on tonight?

DEEP-FRYER: She works Tuesdays.

FOOD PREP: Not Bianca.

DEEP-FRYER: We got crazy energy.

FOOD PREP: She's really gonna miss you when the—

Boooooooooo**oooooom** …

DEEP-FRYER: **Noooo**, aftershock.

Fatal injury.
Heart exploding.
Eyes closing.

FOOD PREP: You're too young to die.

DEEP-FRYER: Tell my mum … I died doing what I love.

FOOD PREP: Tell my mum I died doing what I love … frying chicken.

DEEP-FRYER: I died doing what I love, frying chicken for thirteen dollars an hour—

FOOD PREP: / You get thirteen an hour?

DEEP-FRYER: What do you get?

FOOD PREP: Twelve.

DEEP-FRYER: Me cook. You mayo bitch.

FOOD PREP: That's so—

DEEP-FRYER: / I'm following the bright light.

FOOD PREP: You taught me everything I know.

DEEP-FRYER: Here take this.

FOOD PREP: Your glove.

DEEP-FRYER: I want you to take it.
And treat her well.
Even though the button's a bit broken.
You know don't smash.
Just give it a—

SHIFT MANAGER: / What's happening with order one-five-one? What **are you doing?**

FOOD PREP: **Sorry.**

SHIFT MANAGER: [*to* KIOSK] The kitchen is a high-risk area so it's important— You've completed the safety modules?

KIOSK *nods head yes.*

SHIFT MANAGER: Do you have any questions?

KIOSK *shakes head no.*

DEEP-FRYER: I've had like three dexies and a Red Bull and a No-Doz and at this point in time and space I feel like a fucking machine. I am a gun. I am a helicopter. I'm charged. I'm charged up. I'm like super charged. I'm gonna kill this shift. I'm gonna just [*Miming killing the shift*] I'm a one man franchise, I could be like … like I could totally be like …
[*Running to drive-thru …*] Hi, how can I help you?
[*Running to kitchen …*] Batter the chicken. Batter the chicken.
[*Running to drive-thru …*] That will be blah blah blah.
[*Running to kitchen …*] Put the chicken in the fryer. Fry. Fry. Fry.
[*Running to front counter …*] Hey I'm a customer and gimmie gimmie yummy yummies.
[*Running to kitchen …*] Fry. Fry. Fry.

Beat.

Okay. Okay, okay, okay. Focus. Okay. Fuck, marry, kill … okay … fuck marry kill the deep-fryer, humidified holding cabinet and … and …
The heated holding cabinet.

FOOD PREP: What's the humidified holding …

DEEP-FRYER: It keeps the buns humid. The buns have to be humid.

FOOD PREP: How do you—

DEEP-FRYER: / Because I've tapped into the frequency of the machines. I'm androfied.

FOOD PREP: Du—

DEEP-FRYER: / Shut your mouth. Listen to what they're trying to say …

Long beat.

FOOD PREP: I can't—

DEEP-FRYER: / Listen …

REGULAR: I just feel like tonight was going to be symbolic of everything that I've achieved in my life so far and my schooling and reaching new like milestones in my development and a way to really celebrate … celebrate everything with my peers.

SHIFT MANAGER: What's happening with order one-five-one?

REGULAR: It seems so cruel.

DEEP-FRYER: Block out all the noise. You know all this AI shit's getting real.

FOOD PREP: I—

DEEP-FRYER: / Shhhhh.

Beat.

LITERAL DEEP-FRYER: This is the voice of the deep-fryer.
Not my real voice.
My real voice is all gurgles and hisses.
I began in a manufacturing plant far away from here.
I arrived in bits
then was constructed into a whole thing.
I am a deep abyss.
I swallowed a ring once.
One day I will break.
I'll go into electrical waste
and return to my component parts
eventually decomposing into smaller and smaller parts
slowly over a long period of time.
I swallow birds whole

turning their wings to crispy goldenness.
Chickens and pigeons
I am part of the process
turning something from an alive thing
the flapping and beating and breathing
into the meat thing
into its component parts
into something uniform
something that can be assembled.

FOOD PREP: I can't hear anything.

DEEP-FRYER: I've had three dexies and a Red Bull and a No-Doz.
Look.
Burger-bun boobs.
Like little tiny pillows.

REGISTER TWO: Hi, thanks for waiting. What can I get for you? Unfortunately we don't have the Twister anymore.

Beat.

It was our best burger option by far.

Beat.

Oh trust me, I've contacted them about it.

SHIFT MANAGER: What's happening with order one-five-one?

REGISTER ONE: **Mike. Hello. Mike.**

REGISTER TWO: **I know it's devastating.**

SHIFT MANAGER: In a minute. Someone can't open a **frickin'** box of bread.

DEEP-FRYER: **Whoa.**

KIOSK: I'm thirteen.

Beeping stops.

DEEP-FRYER: **This is fucked in the head. This is totally fucked in the head.**

DRIVE: **This is fucked in the head. This is totally fucked in the head.** I mean it's fine. Everything's completely and totally fine and going to be okay.

A REST BREAK ALLOWS AN EMPLOYEE TO REST FOR A SHORT PERIOD OF TIME DURING WORK HOURS

An air horn blows, which means the performers have a break.

They act as though they are elite athletes preparing for a comp.

Stretching, orange slices, spraying water into their mouths.

They could say things in the vein of 'we got this', or anything that generates the necessary hype in preparation for ...

There is the sound of an air horn, which means we resume.

WORK, BUT GIVE IT ALL YOU GOT

The time is 7:48 p.m. The same nothing song plays.

Everyone is wearing masks.

Action syncs up.

EVERYONE: Hi, thanks for waiting. What can I get you?
I've got the Ultimate Box.
What would you like for your first side?
You get two.
The gravy's not gluten free. Sorry about that.
We can't do mash by itself.
Sorry.
What would you like for your drink?
Pepsi.
Drive through to the next window.

Long beat.

Thanks. Have a good night.

DRIVE: [*to* FOOD PREP] Can you help me with the bins?

FOOD PREP: Sure.

DRIVE *and* FOOD PREP *take off their masks and take out the bins.*

DRIVE: I know you think I'm being dramatic.
But you don't—

EVERYONE: [*except for* DRIVE *and* FOOD PREP] / Hi.

FOOD PREP: I don't think that.

DRIVE: I am being dramatic—

EVERYONE: [*except for* DRIVE *and* FOOD PREP] / Thanks.

FOOD PREP: Nah. It's just like work's work. It sucks, but it's also not like horrible or—

EVERYONE: [*except for* DRIVE *and* FOOD PREP] Thanks for waiting.

FOOD PREP: We try to make it as un-sucky as possible.

DRIVE: But—

EVERYONE: [*except for* DRIVE] / What …

DRIVE: This guy just—

EVERYONE: [*except for* DRIVE *and* FOOD PREP] / I've got the Ultimate Box.

FOOD PREP: What?

DRIVE: A customer … nothing. He was just rude. Annoying customer blah blah blah. I just don't want to be working here when the world ends.

FOOD PREP: I think we'll know when it's about to happen and have time to organise like a big end of the world party where we get to say goodbye to all our loved ones and eat our favourite foods.

DRIVE: What if we keep thinking that we have a little bit more time and a little bit more time and a little bit more time and then the world just fizzles out. And I die with this headset on. Oh my god, I die in this hat.

FOOD PREP: We better go back.

FOOD PREP *and* DRIVE *come back from taking out the bins.*

DRIVE: Yeah.
I think about …

REGISTER TWO: **I think about** that time in your car after work and the way you—

REGULAR: / It's kidney.
I saw it online.

REGISTER ONE: How do you know that?

REGULAR: Online.

REGISTER ONE: Do you like research chicken kidneys in your free time or—

REGULAR: / Oh my god why does it matter. It came up. A guy found what he thought was chicken brain and someone replied to the video explaining how it was actually a kidney. It probably came up because I hang out with you two all the time, and you talk about work all the time and—
I need to pee.

REGULAR *gets out of the car.*

REGISTER ONE: Dramatic.

DEEP-FRYER: I stop being a machine and I think about how my mum does a lot right. She's an absolute legend. She can get real stressed out as well but. I try to like help out and like help her and stuff. Just try to help her feel kinda … everyone likes to feel like nice, like they got good people around them. We do this thing, every friday night, just me and Mum go out for dinner. And the other Friday I was on the train with her—well, I feel like there was a moment and I was like, this … this moment … is like the last time that I will feel like a kid.

Beat.

Okay. So she's like 'What would you like for dinner?'

FOOD PREP: [*in a really bad mum voice*] What would you like for dinner, honey pie?

DEEP-FRYER: Oh my god, my mum does not sound **like that.**

FOOD PREP: **Sorry.**

DEEP-FRYER: Actually kinda offensive.

FOOD PREP: I'll—

DEEP-FRYER: Take it seriously.

FOOD PREP: I'll take it seriously.

DEEP-FRYER: Anyway, I just got this haircut and I asked the guy, just like short back and sides.
He cut way too much length off and I told my mum this and she's like—

FOOD PREP *becomes* DEEP-FRYER'S MUM.

DEEP-FRYER'S MUM: / I think he did take too much length off.
DEEP-FRYER: I told you. And it's not even. This side's like way shorter.
DEEP-FRYER'S MUM: I'll fix it when we get home.
DEEP-FRYER: He took way too much length off.
DEEP-FRYER'S MUM: Don't worry honey. It will grow back.
DEEP-FRYER: And then she runs her fingers through my hair.
Yeah. It just reminded me of— you know. Maybe I'll miss that. It's hard taking care of someone who takes care of you.

The same nothing music becomes a version of the same nothing music that you can slow dance to.

KIOSK *dances with* DRIVE. REGISTER ONE *dances with* SHIFT MANAGER. REGULAR *dances with* DEEP-FRYER. FOOD PREP *dances with* REGISTER TWO.

Beeping starts.

FOOD PREP: Something's beeping?
DEEP-FRYER: Fuck … I forgot about the tenders.
SHIFT MANAGER: What's happening **with order one-five-one—**
FOOD PREP: / **Yeah sorry, I'm** just getting some more buns—
REGISTER ONE: **Mike. Hello. Mike.**
REGISTER TWO: **I know it's totally devastating.**
SHIFT MANAGER: In a minute. Someone can't open a **frickin'** box of bread.
DEEP-FRYER: **Whoa.**
DRIVE: **I can't hear you.**
DEEP-FRYER: **There's kids around.**
KIOSK: **I'm thirteen.**
DRIVE: **Can you move** your umm face closer to the …
SHIFT MANAGER: [*to* REGISTER ONE] Just tell them that we don't serve coffee.
DRIVE: The … the talk box thing.
REGISTER ONE: **They said they wanted to talk to a manager.**
REGISTER TWO: **The closest thing we have would probs have to be the …**
They replaced it with the Crunch Twister but it's really not the same as the OG Twister.

DEEP-FRYER: This is fucked in the head. This is totally fucked in the head.

REGISTER ONE: I think I need to not be here.

A REST BREAK ALLOWS AN EMPLOYEE TO REST FOR A SHORT PERIOD OF TIME DURING WORK HOURS

An air horn blows, which means the performers have a break.

Beat.

If anyone is still wearing a mask they take it off.

Beat.

Everyone lies face down on the ground.

There is the sound of an air horn, which means we resume.

WORK, BUT THIS AIN'T YOUR FIRST RODEO

The time is 7:48 a.m. The same office version of the same nothing song plays.

SHIFT MANAGER: The truth is … This has never been a high performing store. High performing stores win merch like t-shirts, socks, maybe hats … but that's … This job is more of a stepping-stone job for me, so it doesn't even— It's not like future employers are gonna look at the KPIs.

Beat.

They don't look at the KPIs, do they?
My dad thought it would be good for me to get some work experience, start building my resume early, work ethic.
I think the future I want.
I have growth mindset.
I am drinking water from a little plastic cup.
It is cold.
I have—

BOSS: / Do you have those really important business documents I asked for?

SHIFT MANAGER: No. I mean, not yet. But umm … I'll get them to you.

BOSS: What do I pay you to do?

SHIFT MANAGER: Work?

BOSS: You make me feel like I've employed someone who is just a pile of dogs stuffed inside a suit.

SHIFT MANAGER: No.

BOSS: I've got to go. But I want those really important business documents on my desk before five.

SHIFT MANAGER: I wanted to talk to you actually.

BOSS: To me?

SHIFT MANAGER: Yes. We've got a bit of a problem.

BOSS: Is it the Special Ranch Sauce?

SHIFT MANAGER: No—

BOSS: / Has someone done something wrong?

SHIFT MANAGER: I don't think so.

BOSS: Is it the campaign about the … what is it.

SHIFT MANAGER: Climate change?

BOSS: No, the …

SHIFT MANAGER: Mental health?

BOSS: No the … something to do with those uhh … small … and weak …
Children.

SHIFT MANAGER: It's not really—

REGULAR *becomes* MARKET RESEARCHER.

MARKET RESEARCHER: / Do you have a minute.

SHIFT MANAGER: Sorry, who are you?

MARKET RESEARCHER: I'm a market researcher.
Do you have a minute? It's about the new sauce.

BOSS: The Special Ranch Sauce?

MARKET RESEARCHER: The cheesy sauce.

BOSS: I didn't know we were doing that.

MARKET RESEARCHER: It was your idea.
Focus groups are—

BOSS: / They don't like it?

MARKET RESEARCHER: They're not a fan of the texture.

BOSS: We can change the texture.

SHIFT MANAGER: Sorry, but—

MARKET RESEARCHER: / They're saying that it's both watery but simultaneously dry. They used the wooooords [*checking*] 'severe dryness of mouth'.

BOSS: Can something be watery and dry?

SHIFT MANAGER: Maybe it's like—

BOSS: / Sorry sweetheart, it's not really your department.

SHIFT MANAGER: Sorry.

MARKET RESEARCHER: They also said it was fizzy.

BOSS: Is it meant to be fizzy?

MARKET RESEARCHER: No.

BOSS: Why is it fizzy?

MARKET RESEARCHER: We don't know.

BOSS: Can we make it less fizzy?

MARKET RESEARCHER: We don't know.

SHIFT MANAGER: Sorry, but could we—

BOSS: / Yes, about the children.

SHIFT MANAGER: No it's about umm, working conditio—

BOSS: / Shhhhhh. Back to this cheesy sauce conundrum. It shouldn't be fizzy. Right?

MARKET RESEARCHER: It really shouldn't be fizzy. It should be cheesy.

SHIFT MANAGER: There's been a bit of bad press.

BOSS: About the children?

SHIFT MANAGER: No, the umm … Well, there's this franchise.

BOSS: Where?

SHIFT MANAGER: One of the ones in [*the place in which the play is being performed*] has had a—

BOSS: / Is that in Canada? No, don't tell me … A small town in Vermont?

SHIFT MANAGER: No it's—

BOSS: / I think I holidayed there, a ski trip. I got a little taste for the competition and ended up nipping a snowboarder with one of my crampons.

MARKET RESEARCHER: I don't mean to interrupt but we've got the cheesy sauce launch coming up in a couple of weeks and—

SHIFT MANAGER: / It's just it's on the news.

BOSS: The what? New-ooows?

SHIFT MANAGER: The news.

BOSS: News?

SHIFT MANAGER: The news.
BOSS: Send them a merch basket or a chicken or whatever we do.
SHIFT MANAGER: There was a bit of an accid—
BOSS: / Epiphany. We advertise the sauce as a fizzy sauce. A fizzy cheesy sauce. We call it Fizz Wizz.
MARKET RESEARCHER: That's definitely trademarked.
SHIFT MANAGER: The Tongue Puzzler.
BOSS: Sounds sexual.
MARKET RESEARCHER: Tartasia?
We could partner with Disney.
BOSS: Get the marketing team to come up with something better.
I'm gonna have lunch now.
SHIFT MANAGER: But the—
BOSS: / Email me. Where's the **first-aid box?**

Beeping.

SHIFT MANAGER: What?
DEEP-FRYER: **Fuck.**
SHIFT MANAGER: What?

Beeping stops.

DEEP-FRYER: This is totally fucked in the head.

WORK, BUT PICTURE US WITH FLAMES SHOOTING OUT OF OUR EYES

The time is 7:48 p.m. The same nothing song plays.

DRIVE: I'm standing here … I'm standing here … and I'm like hi, thanks for waiting what can I get for you tonight? And my voice is kinda … it's a little higher than how I normally talk. I find that when I talk to customers my voice alway goes like … hi thanks for waiting, like hi thanks for waiting. And they're … the customer … the customer is like, can I get the Ultimate Box? And then I say, so I've got the Ultimate Box. What would you like for your first side?

Beat.

FOOD PREP *becomes* CUSTOMER.

CUSTOMER: **Regular chips.**

DRIVE: **Regular chips.** Is what the customer says. Then I say, what would you like for your second side?

CUSTOMER: **Coleslaw.**

DRIVE: **Coleslaw.**

Drink?

CUSTOMER: **Pepsi Max.**

DRIVE: **Pepsi Max**. Or at least that's what— he definitely said Pepsi Max. And then he winds down his window. And then he taps his card. And then he—

CUSTOMER: / What's this?

DRIVE: And he takes the—

CUSTOMER: / What's this?

DRIVE: He looks like someone's dad.

CUSTOMER: I said what's this.

DRIVE: Sorry, I didn't— One hand is clenched on the steering wheel and the other is hanging out the window.

CUSTOMER: I didn't order a drink.

DRIVE: —

CUSTOMER: So, what did I just get charged for?

DRIVE: An Ultimate Box. The drink's in the deal.

CUSTOMER: I'm gonna need a refund.

DRIVE: It's in the deal so I think—

CUSTOMER: / Do you think? I don't have time for this. Can I get my receipt please?

DRIVE: Yeah uh …

Beat.

Sorry, the machine's just …

CUSTOMER: I can't believe this. I can't bloody believe this.

DRIVE: Sorry.

CUSTOMER: Dumb—

REGULAR: / Hey is my tongue green?

REGISTER TWO: Here's a thought, right …

As a company you cannot go around saying you're in possession of, well a bunch of bodies. That we like rent for like however many hours. Like I pay you and in return you give me an hour of your life.

Like I feel like a manager can't really go around saying oh yeah I kinda oversee someone else's pissing and shitting, that's my job.

REGISTER ONE: I've gotten in trouble for not putting on the fake smile, nice voice, open body language, all that.

REGISTER TWO: I'm kinda in charge of how someone looks, what someone says, how someone moves.

REGISTER ONE: But they don't understand that some male customers take that as meaning something like … you know, you don't wanna smile at some creep. It's definitely not the worst thing in the world.

REGISTER TWO: It's not the worst thing in the world. I used to work for my uncle's friend—

DRIVE: / I just get this feeling like, ummm …

REGISTER TWO: … in this cafe and he would full-on scream …

REGISTER ONE: I just feel like if I had this Grill'd job—

REGISTER TWO: / Like you don't know how to sweep a floor. You're an idiot da da da.

DRIVE: Like everyone's coping really well, but I'm not coping really well. And—

REGISTER ONE: / Sorry, I didn't see you there.

DRIVE: **Hi, thanks for waiting. What can I get you?**

REGISTER ONE: **Hi, thanks for waiting. What can I get you?** Actually, no.

REGISTER ONE *exits.*

SHIFT MANAGER: How are the tenders going?

DRIVE: Ultimate Box.

DEEP-FRYER: Golden.

DRIVE: Would you like a drink with that?

SHIFT MANAGER: Order one-four-eight.

DRIVE: Please proceed to the next window.

FOOD PREP: What.

DEEP-FRYER: Mattress fire.

REGISTER ONE *returns with a bottle of kerosene and begins to pour it across the stage.*

REGISTER ONE: It pisses me off when people complain about work. I think it's easier if you don't complain. I think it's easier if you just imagine—

Burning it to the ground until all that remains is a melted plastic bog.

REGISTER TWO: What are you doing?

REGISTER ONE: I've decided to destroy everything.

DRIVE: And then I was just like thanks, have a good night.

REGISTER TWO: I reckon just sit down, take a breather—

REGISTER ONE: / I don't want to breathe.

DRIVE: Or I think I even said great night.

DEEP-FRYER: I once saw a whole pigeon fall into the deep-fryer.

REGISTER TWO: I'm too young to burn alive.

DEEP-FRYER: Like that's dark shit, man.

REGISTER TWO: How could you do that?

REGISTER ONE: How could you stop me from doing this.

DEEP-FRYER: That's staying with me.

REGISTER ONE: Your ghost will be in biro. Mine will be embedded in the foundations—

REGISTER TWO: / Why do you get a fuck off ghost?

REGISTER ONE: Because my ghost will be angry.

REGISTER TWO: Well, I'm gonna have an angry ghost too.

REGISTER TWO *takes the kerosene.*

DEEP-FRYER: Wings and oil and the smell of burnt feathers. Like a living thing is not meant to be deep fried, you know.

REGISTER TWO: Sometimes you can be so selfish. I love you, but sometimes you can steal all the rage and leave nothing for anyone else. Sometimes you dominate other people.

Beat.

Fuck you, chairs.

REGISTER ONE: Fuck you, EFTPOS machine.

REGISTER TWO: Fuck you tiles.

REGISTER ONE: Ugly fucking tiles.

KIOSK: Fuck you, self-service kiosk.

Sorry, is it okay if I—

REGISTER TWO: / Fuck you electronic display signs.

REGISTER ONE: I never liked you.

REGISTER TWO: Fuck you, hats.

FOOD PREP: Big fuck you, hats.
DEEP-FRYER: What the fuck. These are my materials.
REGULAR: Fuck you … sorry I just wanted to join in.
DRIVE: Fuck you, customers.

Beeping.

REGISTER ONE: Oh my god, fuck you, customers.
DRIVE: Fuck you minumum wage.
FOOD PREP: Fuck getting paid less than adults.
DEEP-FRYER: Actually that shit's like fully why.
REGISTER TWO: Fuck managers.
REGISTER ONE: Yeah fuck managers.
REGULAR: Fuck drinking too many frozen Mountain Dews and throwing up in the bush outside.
KIOSK: Fuck modules.
DRIVE: Fuck whoever owns this fucking franchise.
REGISTER ONE: Fuck whoever owns this fucking empire.
DEEP-FRYER: Fuck the Colonel.

Beeping stops.

DRIVE: I just wish I didn't say have a great night.

Everyone is singing from the Employee Handbook as though it is the sheet music for a choir.

EVERYONE: [*singing*]
Hello
And welcome
Welcome to our little family
This is your employee handbook
With everything you need to know
As the newest member of our team
By now you've probably realised it's a pretty tight-knit team
SHIFT MANAGER: Have you read through the employee handbook?

KIOSK *nods head yes.*

EVERYONE: [*singing*]
Our core values are
As stated below

One
Be the best you that you can possibly be

Beat.

Two
Trust in our world famous recipes and secret spice blend

Beat.

Three
Wear your uniforms with pride and never forget your hat or name badge

Beat.

Four
Punctuality
Make sure you have changed into your uniform and washed your hands and put away your personal possessions and done everything you need to do before you clock in

Long beat.

Five
Have fun

SHIFT MANAGER: Do you have any questions?

KIOSK *shakes head no.*

KIOSK: [*as a solo*]
Here at █████ we take your safety and security very very seriously
All of our restaurants are fitted with security cameras
They are also in the freezers
And in the parking lot
Remember that you are being recorded at all times
And if there is a situation where an incident or misconduct took place
The managerial team of your restaurant may review the footage from the security cameras to monitor—

REGULAR *coughs.*

REGULAR: …
Sorry, I …

REGULAR *takes a sip of Mountain Dew.*

REGISTER TWO: All good.
REGULAR: Yeah, sorry.
EVERYONE: [*singing*]
Do not post any photos or videos from inside the restaurant, including those of coworkers, customers, or work events
Do not post photos or videos of employees in uniform
Do not communicate with each other on Facebook
Or Instagram
Or Snapchat
Or anything like that

A REST BREAK ALLOWS AN EMPLOYEE TO REST FOR A SHORT PERIOD OF TIME DURING WORK HOURS

An air horn blows, which means the performers have a break.

Before they have time to do anything at all ...

There is the sound of an air horn, which means we resume.

WORK, ALL DISGUSTING AND GLISTENING IN THE NIGHT

It's 7:53 p.m. The same nothing song plays.

FOOD PREP: We're outta burger buns.
DEEP-FRYER: There's a box in … up there I reckon.
FOOD PREP: You gotta stop doing burger-bun boobs.
DEEP-FRYER: You love burger-bun boobs.
FOOD PREP: They're gonna come for me. And it's you who's wasting all the—

Beeping.

FOOD PREP: Something's beeping?
DEEP-FRYER: Fuck … I forgot about the tenders.
SHIFT MANAGER: What's happening **with order one-five-one—**
FOOD PREP: / **Yeah sorry I'm** just getting some more buns because—

SHIFT MANAGER: / We need to be moving faster.

FOOD PREP: Yep.

DRIVE: **Can you move closer to the speaker.**

REGISTER TWO: **The closest thing we have would probs have to be the …**

REGISTER ONE: **Mike, a customer wants to talk to you.**

SHIFT MANAGER: **We're really behind tonight, team.** We need to pick up the pace.

Where's your hat?

FOOD PREP: I left it at home.

SHIFT MANAGER: It's health and **safety, mate.**

FOOD PREP: **Customers** can't even see me.

SHIFT MANAGER: Health. And. **Saaaffeeettty.**

REGISTER ONE *enters the kitchen.*

REGISTER ONE: **Mike. Mike, a customer wants to talk to—**

SHIFT MANAGER: [*to* KIOSK] / **We wear hats instead of hair nets here,** so it's really important that you remember your hat.

FOOD PREP: Where's the mini knifey **thing.**

REGISTER ONE: **Mike.** Hello. **Mike.**

SHIFT MANAGER: **What.**

FOOD PREP *starts to open the box of buns.*

REGISTER ONE: A customer wants a coffee.

SHIFT MANAGER: We don't do coffee.

REGISTER ONE: **Yeah, I told them that. They won't listen to me.**

REGISTER TWO: **They replaced it with the Crunch Twister but …**

SHIFT MANAGER: **In a minute. Someone can't open a frickin' box of bread.**

DEEP-FRYER: **Whoa.**

REGISTER ONE: **Mike.**

DEEP-FRYER: **Mike**, there's kids around.

KIOSK: I'm thirteen.

FOOD PREP *cuts off their finger with the box cutter.*

Beeping stops.

KIOSK *is the only one who notices.*

KIOSK: Excuse me. **Something's—**
SHIFT MANAGER: / **Can everyone** just shush for one second.
DRIVE: Shit the tenders are burnt.

REGISTER ONE *screams.*

DEEP-FRYER: **Fuck.**
KIOSK: **We should** put it in the freezer.

REGISTER TWO *comes into the kitchen.*

REGISTER TWO: What's going— Oh my god, **are you okay?**
REGISTER ONE: **Obviously not.**
KIOSK: We should put the finger in the freezer.
REGISTER ONE: **Don't touch it.**
DEEP-FRYER: **Talk to me.**
KIOSK: Where are the gloves?
REGISTER TWO: Would it be weird if I took a photo?
KIOSK: [*to* SHIFT MANAGER] **Excuse me?**
REGISTER ONE: **I think it** would be pretty fucking weird.

REGISTER TWO *holds out their phone.*

KIOSK: [*to* SHIFT MANAGER] Where's your first-aid box?
DEEP-FRYER: Are you taking a **photo?**
REGISTER TWO: **No.**
DEEP-FRYER: Can you not?

DRIVE *enters.*

REGISTER TWO: **I'm not.**
REGISTER ONE: **I actually can't.**
DRIVE: **What happened.**
REGISTER TWO: That guy's finger fell off.
REGISTER ONE: **Don't say that.**
DRIVE: **Why are you** all just standing there.
SHIFT MANAGER: I might umm … get a drink of **water.**
DRIVE: **Excuse me.**
DEEP-FRYER: **Bro.**
KIOSK: Where's the first-aid box?

SHIFT MANAGER: It's **umm … umm …**

DEEP-FRYER: **This is fucked in the head. This is totally fucked in the head.**

DRIVE: **This is fucked in the head. This is totally fucked in the head.** [*to* FOOD PREP] I mean it's fine. Everything's completely and totally fine **and going to be okay.**

REGISTER ONE: **Mike, where's the first-aid box?**

SHIFT MANAGER: I think it's in the staff room above the … what's it called … **the water spout …**

REGISTER TWO: **Fountain?**

SHIFT MANAGER: No, the …

REGISTER ONE: **Sink?**

SHIFT MANAGER: **The sink.**

KIOSK *goes to get the first-aid box.*

DRIVE: [*to* FOOD PREP] What happened?

FOOD PREP: I have an oboe lesson **tomorrow.**

DEEP-FRYER: **Jesus.**

DRIVE: Put your arm above your head okay.

REGISTER TWO: **That's so smart.**

DRIVE: **They're getting the** first-aid box. It's gonna be okay.

KIOSK *comes back.* KIOSK *opens the first-aid box.*

KIOSK: It's empty.

DRIVE: What?

KIOSK: You don't have any first aid.

DRIVE: Mike?

SHIFT MANAGER: Umm.

REGISTER ONE: I think I need to not be here.

REGISTER TWO: [*to* REGISTER ONE] You alright.

REGISTER ONE: **I don't know.**

SHIFT MANAGER: **I don't know.**

DRIVE: How can you not know?

SHIFT MANAGER: There's six other shift managers. And a trainee shift manager. And … and the assistant general manager. It's really an assistant general manager **problem.**

DRIVE: **I'm gonna** call an ambulance.

SHIFT MANAGER: Is an ambulance really—

REGISTER TWO: / Man, there's a finger on the—

REGISTER ONE: / Shut up.

DEEP-FRYER: Call the ambulance.

REGISTER TWO: [*to* REGISTER ONE] Close your eyes.

DRIVE: [*to the phone*] **Hi, my friend has had an accident.**

DEEP-FRYER: **It's okay. It's okay.**

SHIFT MANAGER: **Okay**. So now the situation is under control I think it's time we …

DRIVE: [*on the phone*] **Still conscious.**

SHIFT MANAGER: **That we …**

DEEP-FRYER: What?

SHIFT MANAGER: Well there's about ten orders we still need **to**—

DEEP-FRYER: / **Nah.**

DRIVE: **What's this address?**

SHIFT MANAGER: **An ambulance is** on it's way, so let's **take a deep breath and**—

DRIVE: / **Mike, what's the address.**

KIOSK: Two five eight Levet Street.

SHIFT MANAGER: Everyone calm down, take a deep breath and— great, now there's a line in the drive-thru.

DEEP-FRYER: I'm not leaving my friend to **bleed out on the floor.**

REGISTER ONE: **Actually shut up.**

DRIVE: / That's ridiculous. [*Back to phone*] **Sorry, there's been a workplace injury.**

SHIFT MANAGER: **It's not gonna help umm …** [*Searching for name*] It's not gonna help the situation everyone just milling—

DRIVE: / No-one's going back to work.

DEEP-FRYER: Have some respect.

REGISTER TWO: If no-one's going back to work then I'm definitely not going back to work.

Everyone looks at each other for the first time ever.

SHIFT MANAGER: I hate to say this, but you leave me with no other choice … I'm calling the assistant general shift manager.

WORK, THROUGH THE MEDIUM OF NIGHTMARES

It's 7:59 p.m. A nightmare version of the same nothing song plays. FOOD PREP *is wrapped in a silver blanket.*

SHIFT MANAGER: In this moment I felt like … I've never told anyone this before, but every night I dream of work.
Work but everything's submerged in water.
Work but all the customers are bald.
Work but I'm naked.
Work but the walls are dripping in mayonnaise.
Work but I'm running late and I can't find my name badge.
Work but I'm running late and I can't find my pants.
Work but my entire family is here.
Work but it's like a kinda hybrid of school and work.
Work but I'm really old.
Work but I'm really young.
Work but I can't breathe.
Work but all the food is made out of sand.
Work but out the back is all these potatoes and chickens and I have to like catch the chickens and pluck them and take their insides out and I don't know how to do it and everyone's just staring and laughing at me.
Work but—

KIOSK *enters wearing a crown.*

KIOSK: Hi Mike.
SHIFT MANAGER: Who are you?
KIOSK: You know who I am.
SHIFT MANAGER: A … an angel?

KIOSK *shakes head no.*

A king?

KIOSK *shakes head no.*

A … dad?
KIOSK: I'm the boss of everyone.

SHIFT MANAGER: The assistant general manager?

KIOSK *shakes head no.*

The general manager?

KIOSK *nods head yes.*

Why are you here?

KIOSK *becomes the* GENERAL MANAGER.

GENERAL MANAGER: I think you know why I'm here Mike.
SHIFT MANAGER: You're going to fire me.
GENERAL MANAGER: I can see that you're struggling.
SHIFT MANAGER: Everything's under control.
GENERAL MANAGER: But it all seems a bit out of control.
SHIFT MANAGER: I can do better.
GENERAL MANAGER: On Monday you received an achievement award.
SHIFT MANAGER: For my KPIs.
GENERAL MANAGER: We'd like it back.

SHIFT MANAGER *hands a crumpled piece of paper from their pocket to* GENERAL MANAGER.

There, there. You're still a valued part of our little family.
You know what I tell myself every morning?
SHIFT MANAGER: —
GENERAL MANAGER: Every morning I wake up and look in the mirror and I slap myself in the face and tell myself …
I say …

Beat.

All I ask is that today you do the best work of your entire life.

Beat.

You know who says that?
SHIFT MANAGER: —
GENERAL MANAGER: Steve Jobs.

GENERAL MANAGER *eats* FOOD PREP*'s severed finger.*

Steve Jobs said that.

GENERAL MANAGER *exits.*

SHIFT MANAGER *follows.*

SHIFT MANAGER: Wait. Wait, I want to go with you.

NOT WORK

It's 8:02 p.m. The same nothing song plays.

DRIVE: I'm gonna turn this off.

The song stops.

REGISTER TWO: Hey, can I get a lift with you?

REGISTER ONE: Yeah, but I'm picking up Milo.

REGULAR: Can I come? My mum's gonna scream my head off when I get home.

DRIVE: [*to* KIOSK] How are you getting home.

KIOSK: I have to wait for my mum to pick me up.

DRIVE: I'll wait with you.

KIOSK: Thanks.

DRIVE: I'm not gonna leave you alone after the—
You okay?

KIOSK: My mum's a nurse so I don't really care about gross stuff.

DRIVE: On my way home I get discount-end-of-the-day sushi and a six pack of the cheapest beer and I fall asleep thinking about everything I could have said to that guy who called me a dumb bitch.

DEEP-FRYER: [*to* KIOSK *mouth full of chips*] Wanna chip?

KIOSK: What?

DEEP-FRYER: Chip.

KIOSK: Yeah.

DEEP-FRYER: Do you like the sauce?

KIOSK: Yeah.

DRIVE: Tomorrow at work the 'dumb bitch guy' comes back.

DEEP-FRYER: It's all the sauces mixed together.

DRIVE: So I spit in his Ultimate Box.

DEEP-FRYER: It's a mega sauce.

KIOSK: It's good.

DEEP-FRYER: **Small wins.**

DRIVE: **Small wins.**
DEEP-FRYER: You good, Fifi.
KIOSK: My name's not Fifi. They just gave me this name badge out of lost and found.

Everyone starts to clean up the stage.

DEEP-FRYER: Oh yeah, they do that. So what's your name?
KIOSK: It's [*whatever the performer's name is*].
DEEP-FRYER: I'm [*whatever the performer's name is*].

As they clean they're having little conversations. They don't talk as their characters but as themselves. So this is unscripted.

Except for FOOD PREP ...

FOOD PREP: So after this moment
The history of this franchise
That's all great big gulping boomingness
My finger is reattached
My oboe is sold on Facebook Marketplace
The Retail and Fast Food Workers Union
I get really into it
I try to organise
The main difficulty is everyone's so temporary and casual and young and tryna deal with every single thing that ever existed
I learn how to arrive on time and leave a little later
I learn how to be still for six hours
A year after this incident someone burns their hand with hot oil
The manager on shift says to treat it with mustard
Wounds are now dressed and bathed in mustard
The Retail and Fast Food Workers Union
Makes a Facebook post
About the mustard
We engrave eulogies and love letters to each other
In the bathrooms
Which are painted over forever and ever
After the Facebook post
Staff protest outside this franchise
For living wages

Safer working conditions
We make banners
The union helps take [redacted] to court for failing to give workers their paid ten-minute break that they legally require every four hours
I leave
Because I start losing shifts when I turn twenty-three
I work
I work while I see older people retire and question who they are without work
This place where I worked is demolished and becomes a freeway to make it quicker for people to get to work
They do not build a monument to what once existed
made of empty Mountain Dew bottles and chicken bones
I remember this smell for the rest of my life
The moments will fold into each other
And my hands will remember these movements forever and ever.

FOOD PREP *joins everyone else. Everyone is packing up, doing what needs to be done. Resetting the stage. They are operating as a well-oiled machine, working their butts off, earning their money, pushing through, pumping it out, moving on up, work bitch work.*

END

CANBERRA YOUTH THEATRE PRESENTS

WORK, BUT THIS TIME LIKE YOU MEAN IT

BY HONOR WEBSTER-MANNISON

WORLD PREMIERE
20 - 29 SEPTEMBER 2024
THE COURTYARD STUDIO – CANBERRA THEATRE CENTRE

CAST

SHIFT MANAGER	TOM BRYSON
DRIVE	QUINN GOODWIN
FOOD PREP	STERLING NOTLEY
DEEP FRYER	MATTHEW HOGAN
REGISTER ONE	KATHLEEN DUNKERLEY
REGISTER TWO	EMMA PIVA
KIOSK	GEORGIE BIANCHINI
REGULAR	HANNAH CORNELIA

CREATIVE TEAM

DIRECTOR	LUKE ROGERS
SET & COSTUME DESIGNER	KATHLEEN KERSHAW
LIGHTING & VIDEO DESIGNER	ETHAN HAMILL
SOUND DESIGNER & COMPOSER	PATRICK HAESLER
PRODUCTION STAGE MANAGER	RHILEY WINNETT

ACKNOWLEDGEMENTS

We greatly acknowledge the support of the ACT Government through artsACT, and Ainslie and Gorman Arts Centres. This production is supported by Canberra Theatre Centre, as part of a commitment to nurturing the young and emerging artists of the ACT.

Honor Webster-Mannison was the winner of the 2022 Emerging Playwright Commission, generously supported by Holding Redlich.

THE VOICE OF YOUTH EXPRESSED THROUGH CHALLENGING AND INTELLIGENT THEATRE

Canberra Youth Theatre is one of Australia's leading youth arts organisations, and a hub for brave, authentic, and challenging new works. From the initial spark of an idea, to the first day of rehearsal, to the final bow of production, we drive social transformation through a dynamic artistic practice and an inclusive youth-led approach to creative expression. We empower our young people to advocate for both their social and artistic agency, and to tell brand new stories for every new generation.

For over 50 years Canberra Youth Theatre has been a vital organisation in the local and national arts scene. We have created new works in major theatres, public spaces, and national cultural institutions – touring both nationally, and internationally. We have built a reputation for being at the forefront of youth-led artistic practice. Our community continues to thrive throughout the world, as both innovative artists and more broadly, deeply empathetic collaborators. We pass the torch to our young artists, and in doing so foster an environment of professional behaviour, a practice of empathetic witnessing, and a belief in artistic excellence.

From Debra Oswald's now Australian classic *Dags*, and works by writers Tommy Murphy, Mary Rachel Brown, Lachlan Philpott, Angela Betzien, Liv Hewson, Ross Mueller, Emily Sheehan, Jessica Bellamy, Cathy Petocz, Julian Larnach, Joanna Richards, Honor Webster-Mannison and Tasnim Hossain, we have nurtured new voices and commissioned professional artists to create works which represent the voice of youth at its most exciting. Our work fosters not only writers, but develops performers, designers, directors, theatremakers, and cultural leaders, who help bring these stories to life.

Our legacy speaks to the evolving needs and aspirations of Canberra's generations of emerging artists, adapting to new modes of theatre-making, questions of national and cultural identity, and the ever-present need for young people to create, connect, and collaborate in a theatre where their voice is key. We continue to strive to create innovative, accessible and challenging opportunities for young people to access and engage in professional-quality artistic experiences.

The future of the arts begins with youth.

Canberra Youth Theatre acknowledges the Ngunnawal people as traditional custodians of the lands on which we collaborate, share stories, and create art. We recognise all other First Nations peoples and families with connection to the ACT and region. We pay our respects to their Elders past, present and emerging. Sovereignty was never ceded.

HONOR WEBSTER-MANNISON
PLAYWRIGHT

Pageboy to your unruly subconscious, Honor Webster-Mannison is a performer, theatre-maker and playwright, currently based on Wurundjeri Country. Honor uses collaborative devising and writing methods to make experimental performance work. Their practice explores fluid spaces where various theatrical elements such as text, design, sound and movement emerge simultaneously. Performance works that Honor has co-created include *Deep Breath In* (Dead Puppets Society's LAB); *Sludge Bank* (Metro Arts' Young Artist Forum); *This Fantastic Plastic Planet* (Backbone Festival); and *Sometime's It's Hot Like the Sun* (Festival of Australian Student Theatre). Honor's short work *Bottlefeeders* was staged by the Australian Theatre for Young People as part of the 2017 Voices Project. They completed their Masters of Theatre (Writing) at the Victorian College of the Arts in 2022. In 2023, Honor received the Canberra Youth Theatre Emerging Playwright Commission to write *Work, But This Time Like You Mean It.*

PLAYWRIGHT'S NOTE

When I first started writing, I wrote about semi-suburban-industrial spaces, about empty lots with the long grass and the overturned shopping trolleys, about people's bodies mutating into infrastructure. When I started writing this play, I collected photos of abandoned spaces, and when I finished writing this play I found a small herd of goats in an empty lot on my way home from work. After spending the day workshopping the play at Canberra Youth Theatre, I walked back to my hotel room through the Civic Centre and wrote about how much the shops have carved the space. I read an article about a sonic anti-loitering device called The Mosquito. The device emits an uncomfortable, painful sound only audible to people under twenty-five, including babies. The Mosquito was installed in a Queensland shopping centre, under recommendation of the police, and was in operation for ten years. When the device was installed younger employees started complaining of lasting headaches and ear pains. The Mosquito was removed after two years of pressure from a solicitor on the basis that the device violated anti-discrimination laws and the UN Convention on the Rights of the Child. This touches on the corporate domination of space and the fear of teenagers occupying space.

A lot of what happens in this play is true. It is informed by the thoughts and experiences of participants from Canberra Youth Theatre who volunteered their time to workshop the play, conversations with friends about their first jobs, and reading articles, Reddit threads and particularly Stuart Tannock's book *Youth at Work: The Unionized Fast-food and Grocery Workplace.* One 'solution' for unwanted teen loitering is to decrease youth joblessness. Young people predominantly work unstable, low-waged, low-status and 'dead-end' jobs while some of the richest companies in the world profit from these poor labour conditions and low wages. KFC Australia's website states that ninety percent of team members are under the age of twenty-five. For McDonald's, seventy percent of restaurant employees are in secondary or tertiary education. The junior wage is a stark example of the way society values young people's labour less than adult labour. And although young workers are more likely to face wage theft and have their legal working conditions violated, they are far less likely to be in a union than workers above the age of twenty-five.

Recently, there have been significant developments in Australia in campaigning for the rights of young workers as well as grassroots unionisation in the fast-food industry. In 2016 the Retail and Fast Food Workers Union (RAFFWU) was established in response to the lack of a member-led union prepared to actively fight for the rights of retail and fast-food workers. Prior to this, the only available union for retail and fast-food workers was the Shop, Distributive and Allied Employees' Association (SDA), which made agreements resulting in wage loss and poorer working conditions for employees. The Young Workers Centre, which provides various resources including legal support for young workers, is campaigning to end junior wages, with their campaign 'Fair Wages All Ages'. These developments suggest possible futures in which young people's relationship to work can be more than one of providing cheap disposable labour, and instead one of agency.

A couple of weeks after I finish writing this play I go to McDonald's and have a conversation with an employee about the rise and fall of Shaker-Fries. I eat in and feel a deeply familiar experience of nothing discernible. I think about documenting what happens in places that are transitory. The histories of adolescence and food chains are not meant to be recorded. This is not meant to be a site of importance, a place of power or resistance.

I would like to give special thanks to everyone at Canberra Youth Theatre who participated in workshopping and developing this play; without them this work would not be possible.

Honor Webster-Mannison

DIRECTOR'S NOTE

Everyone remembers their first job – no matter how much some might want to forget it. It's a rite of passage, simultaneously teaching you important, character-building life lessons, whilst also careening you straight into an existential crisis about the terrifying meaningless of life. Namely, seemingly wasting your young life away, one shift at a time, for significantly less than minimum wage.

Winner of Canberra Youth Theatre's 2022 Emerging Playwright Commission, Honor pitched us a darkly surreal comedy about young people's first experiences in the workplace. They have delivered an unhinged deep-fryer-dive into deeply human relationships, forged within the most alienating of circumstances. In this 'could be any one of them' fast food restaurant, the days never seem to end, and the work never seems to stop. For these teenagers who are stuck in a work-life timey-wimey loop, bathed in neon light and the all-pervading odour of chip fat work becomes a place to interrogate big existential questions about ambition, bodily autonomy, personal identity.

Work, But... it's a completely unhinged, chaotic exploration of the universal rite of passage of first jobs. Here is an absurd world filled with authority figures, power dynamics, attendance, uniforms and work-ethics, where many of the staff are not yet adults, but through darkly humorous camaraderie, are suddenly expected to be.

This production is the culmination of a two-year creative journey between Honor and dozens of emerging artists from Canberra Youth Theatre. Each year, the Emerging Playwright Commission, generously supported by law firm Holding Redlich, nurtures ambitious new plays from first ideas through to full productions. The winning playwright works closely with artists at Canberra Youth Theatre throughout the writing process, to ensure that the work authentically represents the young voices at its core.

Canberra Youth Theatre has long punched above its weight in the ACT theatre scene as a leading producer of adventurous, high-quality productions of urgent new plays for young people. Talented young artists are supported by experienced professionals to create surprisingly mature productions that tackle big ideas with all the fearlessness, curiosity and disrespect for authority that you might expect from a company that champions the voice of youth.

Luke Rogers

CREATIVE TEAM

LUKE ROGERS
DIRECTOR

Luke Rogers is a theatre director, actor, producer, and the Artistic Director and CEO of Canberra Youth Theatre. Luke holds a Master of Fine Arts in Cultural Leadership (2024) and a Graduate Diploma of Dramatic Arts in Directing (2012) from the National Institute of Dramatic Art (NIDA), and a Bachelor of Arts in Performance from Theatre Nepean - University of Western Sydney (2002). As part of his MFA in Cultural Leadership, Luke undertook an international research placement with The National Theatre of Scotland. In 2023, he was awarded the Freddie J Gibson Fellowship to explore youth arts practices across the UK and Ireland. Luke regularly sits on industry panels and advisory groups for government, advocacy organisations and peak bodies. Other positions have included Artistic Director of Stories Like These, Resident Studio Artist at Griffin Theatre Company, Theatre Manager of New Theatre, and Artistic Director of The Spare Room. Directing credits include: *Rosieville*, *The Trials*, *How To Vote*, *Dags*, *Two Twenty Somethings Decide Never To Be Stressed About Anything Ever Again Ever*, *Little Girls Alone in the Woods*, *Normal*, *Possibility*, and *Collapse* (Canberra Youth Theatre); *Mary Stuart* and *Collected Stories* (Chaika Theatre / ACT Hub); *In Real Life* (Darlinghurst Theatre Company); *Blink*, *MinusOneSister*, *Fireface*, *The Last Five Years* and *The Carnivores* (Stories Like These); *Play House* (NIDA); *The Pillowman*, *Waiting For Godot*, *Don Juan in Soho*, *Art is a Weapon*, *After The End* and *Blasted* (New Theatre); *100 Reasons For War*, *Love and Information*, *Spring Awakening*, *A Midsummer Night's Dream*, *Shakespeare's Women* and *Shoot/Get Treasure/Repeat* (AFTT); *Lysistrata*, *The Burial At Thebes*, *Pool (No Water)*, *4.48 Psychosis* and *Eyes To The Floor* (Sydney Theatre School); *A Midsummer Night's Dream* and *Mr Marmalade* (CQUniversity); *Macbeth*, *Cyberbile* and *Embers* (AIM Dramatic Arts); and *Two Weeks With The Queen* (Mountains Youth Theatre). Tour Director: *The Witches* (Griffin Theatre Company). Assistant Director: *Eight Gigabytes of Hardcore Pornography* (Griffin Theatre Company / Perth Theatre Company); *Story of the Red Mountains* (NIDA); *The Boys* (Griffin Theatre Company / Sydney Festival); *Steel Magnolias* (Blackbird Productions / Australian Tour); *Assassins*, *The Crucible* (New Theatre).

KATHLEEN KERSHAW
SET & COSTUME DESIGNER

Kathleen Kershaw is a set and costume designer for live performance and film. Kathleen completed studies at NIDA in 2022, graduating with a Bachelor of Fine Arts in Design for Performance. Through her studies she was Costume Designer for *Picnic at Hanging Rock* and Set and Costume Designer for *Prem Patr*, which has since toured in India and had development with National Theatre of Parramatta. Since graduation set and costume design credits include: *Good Works* and *Terror* (Mill Theatre Dairy Road); *You Can't Tell Anyone* (Canberra Youth Theatre); *King Lear* (Echo Productions); *Crime and Punishment* and *The Girl Who Glows* (The Street Theatre), *Mary Stuart* (Chaika Theatre / ACT Hub). Costume Design: *Loot* (New Theatre). Set Design: *Rockspeare 1H6* (Mill Theatre Dairy Road).

ETHAN HAMILL
LIGHTING & VIDEO DESIGNER

Ethan Hamill is a live event and theatre practitioner specialising in lighting and video design and lighting programming. In 2023, Ethan graduated from the National Institute of Dramatic Art (NIDA) with a Bachelor of Fine Arts in Technical Theatre and Stage Management. Ethan spends most of his time working across Sydney's theatre and live event scenes working on a wide range of shows. He strives to keep up with new and emerging technologies and to incorporate these into his work. Ethan's recent credits include: Lighting Programmer for the Sydney season of *Cost of Living*, Lighting Supervisor for *Golden Blood*, the *RBG: Of Many, One* 2024 tour and Lighting Operator for *Dracula* (Sydney Theatre Company); Lighting Programmer for *The Dismissal: An Extremely Serious Musical Comedy* (Squabbalogic); Lighting Designer for *Rosieville*, *You Can't Tell Anyone*, *The Trials*, and Video Designer for *How To Vote!* (Canberra Youth Theatre); Lighting Operator for *Joseph and the Amazing Technicolour Dreamcoat* (Sydney season, 2023); and Lighting Designer for *The Magic Flute* (NIDA).

CREATIVE TEAM

PATRICK HAESLER
SOUND DESIGNER & COMPOSER

Patrick Haesler is an award-winning composer, performer, sound designer and producer from Ngunnawal Country (Canberra). Beginning as a trumpet player, Patrick has since branched into numerous musical fields, drawing influences from jazz and progressive music. He has used his diverse musical experience to compose music and design sound for films, video games and theatre, and was a Resident Artist with Canberra Youth Theatre in 2023. Patrick's theatre credits include work on *The Trials*, *You Can't Tell Anyone*, *Soul Trading* and *Rosieville* (Canberra Youth Theatre). Patrick has released soundtrack albums for many past productions, including his eleventh studio album, the soundtrack for Canberra Youth Theatre's production of *The Trials*, titled *Climate Trials (Original Theatre Soundtrack)*. Patrick's experience with a wide variety of musical genres, ensembles and production techniques make him a versatile creative in the world of music and sound.

RHILEY WINNETT
PRODUCTION STAGE MANAGER

Rhiley Winnett is an enthusiastic, passionate theatre maker specialising in stage management and a proud member of the Canberra Youth Theatre team. Beginning their career in stage management in 2020, they have since worked on productions including: *Wolf Lullaby* (Echo Theatre); *Dags*, *How to Vote!*, *You Can't Tell Anyone* (Canberra Youth Theatre); *People You May Know* (Lucid Theatre Co.); *I Have No Enemies* (Bare Witness Theatre); and *The Girl Who Glows* (The Street Theatre). Rhiley's time on *Work, But This Time Like You Mean It* has been a massive and fulfilling learning experience, helping them explore new creative avenues and solutions to complicated works speaking to real, contemporary issues. It has been a joy to stage this universal, exciting, unfortunate story of everyday life at its most satirical.

CAST

GEORGIE BIANCHINI
KIOSK

Making their Canberra Youth Theatre debut with *Work, But This Time Like You Mean It*, Georgie's interests and goals have always centred around performance and acting. Having trained with Perform Australia from a young age, Georgie has appeared as Juror 3 in *12 Angry Men* and as Gangster understudy/Ensemble in *Kiss Me, Kate* (Lake Ginninderra College); in *Act Up!* (Canberra Theatre Centre) for three years, and acting with Victoria's Models. Georgie deeply values experiences like this production, believing they create strong connections and relationships between people, and that it is a privilege to share stories through theatre with an audience.

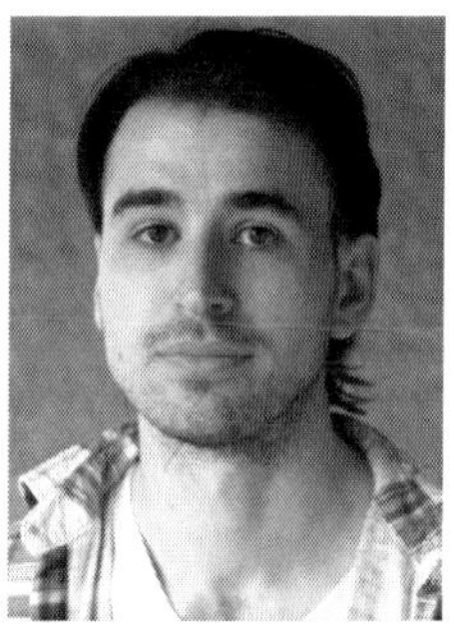

TOM BRYSON
SHIFT MANAGER

Tom is absolutely thrilled to be a part of the *Work, But This Time Like You Mean It* team and to share Honor Webster-Mannison's original and hilarious play. An actor, Tom has trained at Screenwise Film & TV School and The National Acting School. Since debuting professionally as Will in *Fragments* (The Street Theatre), Tom has appeared as James Bryson in *Legacies* (Ribix Productions); Talascar in short film *Cerberus* (dir. Ewout Rohling); and reprised his role as Will in the web series adaptation of *Fragments* (dir. Joshua Koske).

HANNAH CORNELIA
REGULAR

Hannah Cornelia is an actor and writer with a passion for intelligent theatre that reflects young people. She has been an active member of Canberra Youth Theatre as part of their Ambassadors, Young Critics, and Writers Ensemble programs. As an actor, her roles to date have included: Prospero in *The Tempest* and Celia in *As You Like It* (Travelling Players Company, U.S.); Lynette in Debra Oswald's *Dags* (Canberra Youth Theatre); Nell Quickly and ensemble in *Henry V* (Lakespeare); and Margaret in *Sense and Sensibility* (Canberra REP), for which she was nominated for Best Youth Performance at the ACT Ovations Awards. An avid Shakespeare lover, Hannah was also shortlisted for the John Bell Scholarship in 2022. She is enamoured with and excited by Honor Webster-Mannison's writing in *Work, But...* and is positive audiences will share the same sentiment.

CAST

KATHLEEN DUNKERLEY
REGISTER ONE

Kathleen Dunkerley actively participates in the Canberra theatre community as a writer, director, actor, critic, and overall theatre maker. Prior to her role in *Work, But...*, she appeared as Ren in *The Trials* (Canberra Youth Theatre), for which she won the ACT Ovations Award for Outstanding Youth Performance in a Play. She has also appeared as Mary in *The Bald Prima Donna*, Cressida in *Troilus and Cressida*, was a writer and co-director for her debut play *Worms* and part of the writing team for *The Gift of Story* (Daramalan Theatre Company), for which she won a Canberra Area Theatre Award for Best Original School or Youth Production. A former fast food employee, Kathleen resonates deeply with the ethos of this play.

QUINN GOODWIN
DRIVE

Quinn Goodwin is an actor, writer and theatre-maker who has been part of the Canberra theatre community for over ten years. A co-founder of Lucid Theatre Co. with fellow Canberra Youth Theatre Emerge Company alumni, Quinn has previously appeared as Bianca in *People You May Know* (Lucid Theatre Co.), which she also co-created with the company; and in *Possibility* and *How To Vote!* (Canberra Youth Theatre). On screen, Quinn's credits include: Alice in *The Gap Year* (dir. Miahtya Gowland) and Carmen in *1988* (dir. Lilly Endres).

MATTHEW HOGAN
DEEP FRYER

Matt describes himself as an autodidact theatre maker, with a love for the dramatic and an eagerness to entertain. Prior to *Work, But This Time Like You Mean It*, Matt appeared as Tomaz in *The Trials* and Adam in *Dags* (Canberra Youth Theatre); Hamlet in *I Hate Shakespeare*, and Will Parker in *Oklahoma* (Burgmann Anglican School); and King Creon in *Antigone: The Burial at Thebes* (Merici College). Matt sincerely hopes audiences enjoy the show as much as he enjoyed laughing, taunting and working (but like he means it) with his fellow cast and crew.

STERLING NOTLEY
FOOD PREP

Sterling Notley is excited to be making his debut with Canberra Youth Theatre. He has portrayed Macduff in Shakespeare's tragedy *Macbeth*, Roy in Louis Nowra's comedy *Cosi*, and Nathan Detroit in the musical *Guys and Dolls* (Radford Theatre Company), a performance that earned him the Iain Sinclair Award for Excellence in Characterisation. Sterling's performances with Radford Theatre Company in 2023 led to him winning the Tony Harris Performer of the Year Award for Drama. His contributions to theatre are a testament to his passion and hopes that he can continue to perform for years to come.

EMMA PIVA
REGISTER TWO

Emma Piva is excited to be part of this world premiere production of *Work, But This Time Like You Mean It*. She is an active singer/songwriter in the Canberra music scene, opening for acts such as Pacific Avenue, Sophie Edwards and Archie band. With a newfound passion for theatre, she most recently appeared in the principal role of Jo March in *Little Women*, and as Jetsam in *The Little Mermaid* (Canberra Girls Grammar School) for which she was nominated for a Canberra Area Theatre Award. Having never worked as a fast food employee, Emma must admit their admiration for friends who work in hospitality has grown – something she hopes audiences will take away too.

OUR PARTNERS

We gratefully acknowledge the generous support of our partners who are key to the success of our work.

GOVERNMENT PARTNER

Supported by

CREATIVE PARTNERS

PROGRAM PARTNERS

PRODUCTION SPONSORS

MAJOR DONORS

THE
JEREMY SPENCER BROOM
LEGACY

MICHAEL ADENA & JOANNE DALY
THE BAASCH FAMILY
PAUL BIGSBY-CHAMBERLIN
AMY CRAWFORD
STEPHEN FISCHER
MELINDA HILLERY

MERLE KETLEY
TRACY NOBLE
CEDRIC SIMENEL
ANONYMOUS (2)

as of September 2024

If you would like to know more about how you can support us, or are interested in partnering with us, contact **caitlin@canberrayouththeatre.com.au**

STAFF

ARTISTIC DIRECTOR & CEO
LUKE ROGERS

ADMINISTRATOR
HELEN WOJTAS

CREATIVE LEARNING PRODUCER
ANNA JOHNSTONE

MARKETING & ENGAGEMENT MANAGER
CHRISTOPHER CARROLL

FINANCE & STRATEGY MANAGER
LOUISE DAVIDSON

WORKSHOPS COORDINATOR
CHARLOTTE JACKSON

DEVELOPMENT & COMMUNICATIONS COORDINATOR
CAITLIN BAKER

PRODUCTION STAGE MANAGER
RHILEY WINNETT

COMMISSIONED WRITERS

SONIA DODD

BOARD

PETER HOOLIHAN (CHAIR)
ADRIANA LAW (DEPUTY CHAIR)
AMY CRAWFORD
JOANNA ERSKINE
ELLEN HARVEY
CASSANDRA HOOLIHAN
EMMA MACDONALD

WORKSHOP ARTISTS

CAITLIN BAKER
JADE BREEN
ELLA BUCKLEY
ANNA JOHNSTONE
EVA LOXLEY
JUNIPER POTTER
JENA PRINCE
LEAH RIDLEY
RACHEL ROBERTSON
DAYNE SPENCER
LILY WELLING

GORMAN ARTS CENTRE
BATMAN STREET BRADDON ACT 2612
02 6248 5057
INFO@CANBERRAYOUTHTHEATRE.COM.AU

CANBERRAYOUTHTHEATRE.COM.AU

  @canberrayouththeatre